CONSECRATED Life IN THE THIRD MILLENNIUM

Starting afresh from Christ

Instruction

CONGREGATION FOR INSTITUTES OF CONSECRATED
LIFE AND SOCIETIES OF APOSTOLIC LIFE

*All booklets are published thanks to the generous support
of the members of the Catholic Truth Society*

CATHOLIC TRUTH SOCIETY
PUBLISHERS TO THE HOLY SEE

CONTENTS

INTRODUCTION

Contemplating the Splendour of the Face of Christ

1. Contemplating Christ's crucified and glorious face[1] and witnessing to his love in the world, consecrated persons joyfully accept the Holy Father John Paul II's pressing invitation at the beginning of the third millennium *to cast out into the deep*: "Duc in altum!" (*Lk* 5:4). These words, echoed throughout the whole Church have enlivened a powerful new hope, reawakened the desire for a more intense evangelical life, and broken open the horizons of dialogue and mission.

Perhaps today, more than ever, *Jesus' invitation to cast out into the deep* appears as a response to the human drama which is the victim of hate and death. The Holy Spirit is always active in history and can draw from human dramas a discernment of the events which is open to the mystery of mercy and peace among peoples. The Spirit, in fact, from the very troubled nature of the nations calls forth in many the dream of a different world already present among us. John Paul II assures young people of this when he exhorts them to be "sentinels of the dawn" who, strong in the faith, keep watch, awaiting the dawn.[2]

Certainly the dramatic events which have taken place in the world in these recent years have given rise to new and more weighty questions added to those already present, which grow out of a globalised Society. A society with its positive and negative forces in which "not only are technology and economy globalised but also insecurity and fear, crime and violence, injustices and war".[3]

In this situation, *consecrated persons are called by the Spirit to a continual conversion* to give new vigour to the prophetic dimension of their vocation. They who, in fact, are "called to place their very existence at the service of the cause of the Kingdom of God, leaving everything behind and closely imitating the form of life of Jesus Christ,

---

[1] Cf. John Paul II, Post Synodal Apostolic Exhortation *Vita Consecrata*, Rome, 25 March 1996, 14.
[2] John Paul II, Apostolic Letter *Novo Millennio Ineunte*, 6 January 2001, 9.
[3] John Paul II, Talk given to Caritas Italiana (24 November 2001): *L'Osservatore Romano*, 25 November 2001, n.4.

assume a most important teaching role for the whole People of God".[4]

The Holy Father made this expectation clear in his message to the members of the last Plenary Session of our Congregation: "The Church" - he writes - "counts on the continual dedication of this chosen host of her sons and daughters, on their yearning for holiness and upon the enthusiasm of their service to foster and sustain every Christian's striving for perfection and to enhance the common welcoming of neighbour, especially those most in need. In this way, witness is given to the love of Christ among all people".[5]

Walking in the Footsteps of Christ

2. But how do we recognise in the reflection of history and at the present time the signs of the Spirit and *the seeds of the Word*, present now as always in human life and culture?[6] How do we interpret the signs of the times in a reality such as ours in which areas of darkness and mystery abound? As with the disciples on the walk towards Emmaus, the Lord himself must be our travelling companion and grant us his Spirit. Only the Lord, present among us, can help us to fully understand and carry out his word, he can enlighten minds and warm hearts.

"Know that I am with you always, until the end of the world" (*Mt* 28:20). The Risen Lord has remained faithful to this promise. Through the presence of the Holy Spirit, from her very beginnings, the Lord has always been present in the Church, lighting her way, flooding her with graces, giving her the strength to live his word ever more intensely and to carry out the mission of salvation as a sign of the unity of all with God and with each other.[7]

Consecrated life, in its continuous development and experience of new forms, is already in itself an eloquent expression of this very presence, almost a kind of Gospel spread out through the centuries. It appears in fact as a "prolongation in history of a special presence

---

[4] John Paul II, Message to the Plenary Session of The Congregation for Institutes of Consecrated Life and Societies of Apostolic Life (21 September 2001): *L'Osservatore Romano*, 28 September 2001.
[5] *Ibid.*
[6] Cf. *Ad Gentes*, 11.
[7] Cf. *Lumen Gentium*, 1.

of the Risen Lord".[8] With this assurance, consecrated persons must seek a new impetus in Christian living, making it the force which inspires their journey of faith.[9]

Today's world is expecting to see in consecrated men and women the concrete reflection of Jesus' way of acting, of his love for every person without distinction or qualification. It wants to experience that, with the Apostle Paul, it is possible to say: "I still live my human life, but it is a life of faith in the Son of God who loved *me* and gave his life for *me*" (*Gal* 2:20).

Five years after the Apostolic Exhortation "Vita Consecrata"

3. In order to help in the discernment which safeguards this particular vocation, and to support the courageous choice of evangelical witness, at this time, the Congregation for Institutes of Consecrated Life and Societies of Apostolic Life held its Plenary Session 25-28 September 2001.

In 1994 the IX Ordinary Assembly of the Synod of Bishops, having completed the treatment "of the specific identity of the various states of life willed by Jesus for his Church",[10] following the Synods dedicated to the laity and to priests, studied *Consecrated Life and its mission in the Church and in the world*. The Holy Father John Paul II, gathering together the reflections and the hopes of that Assembly, gifted the whole Church with the Post-Synodal Apostolic Exhortation *Vita Consecrata*.

Five years after the publication of this fundamental Document of the Church's Magisterium, our Dicastery, in *Plenary Session*, considered the effectiveness with which it has been received and put into practice within communities and Institutes and in the local Churches.

The Apostolic Exhortation *Vita Consecrata* clearly and profoundly expressed *the Christological and ecclesial dimensions of consecrated life in a Trinitarian theological perspective*, shedding new light on the theology of the following of Christ and of consecration, of communion in community and of mission. It contributed to the

---

[8] *Vita Consecrata*, 19.
[9] Cf. *Novo Millennio Ineunte*, 29.
[10] *Vita Consecrata*, 4.

creation of a new mentality regarding the mission of consecrated life within the people of God. It helped consecrated persons themselves to capture a greater awareness of the grace of their own vocation.

This programmatic document remains the most significant and necessary point of reference guiding the path of fidelity and renewal of Institutes of Consecrated Life and Societies of Apostolic Life while at the same time, allowing for the rising of valid proposals for *new forms of consecrated and evangelical life*. It must continue to be studied, understood and put into practice.

Starting Afresh in Hope

4. The Great Jubilee of 2000, which profoundly involved all forms of consecrated life throughout the world, has had a great impact on the life of the Church. On 2 February 2000, preceded by a prayerful preparation, the Jubilee of Consecrated life was celebrated in all the local Churches.

At the end of the Jubilee Year, in the hope that we might cross the threshold of the new millennium together, the Holy Father sought to summarise the heritage of the Jubilee Celebrations in the Apostolic Letter *Novo Millennio Ineunte*. This text presents, with extraordinary yet predictable continuity, some fundamental themes already mentioned in the Exhortation *Vita Consecrata*: Christ, the centre of life for every Christian,[11] the pastoral practice and teaching on holiness, its demanding character, its *high standard* of ordinary Christian living,[12] the widespread need for spirituality and prayer realised principally in contemplation and in listening to the Word of God,[13] the irreplaceable effects of the sacramental life,[14] the spirituality of communion,[15] and the witness of Love which is expressed in a new *creativity of charity* towards those who suffer, towards a wounded world enslaved in hatred, in a spirit of ecumenical and inter-religious dialogue.[16]

---

[11] Cf. *Novo Millennio Ineunte*, 29.
[12] Cf. *Novo Millennio Ineunte*, 30-31.
[13] Cf. *Novo Millennio Ineunte*, 32-34, 35-39.
[14] Cf. *Novo Millennio Ineunte*, 35-37.
[15] Cf. *Novo Millennio Ineunte*, 43-44.
[16] Cf. *Novo Millennio Ineunte*, 49, 57.

Introduction

The Members of the Plenary, taking as points of departure the elements received from the Apostolic Exhortation and presented by the experience of the Jubilee as well as the call for a new commitment to holiness, highlighted the questions and hopes pointed out by consecrated persons throughout the world, concentrating on the most important aspects. Their intention was not to produce another doctrinal document but rather to help consecrated life enter into the great pastoral guidelines of the Holy Father with the contribution of his authority and of charismatic service to unity and to the universal mission of the Church. A gift which is shared and put into practice with fidelity to the following of Christ through the evangelical counsels and with the strength of charity daily lived in fraternal communion and in a generous apostolic spirituality.

The special Continental Assemblies of the Synod of Bishops which served as preparations for the Jubilee Year have already addressed the hopes and challenges of consecrated life in the context of the local Churches and cultures. The members of the Plenary did not intend to offer another analysis of the situation. More simply, taking into account the present state of religious life and seeking to remain attentive to the guidelines of the Holy Father, they invite consecrated men and women in their particular situation and culture *to focus primarily on spirituality*. Their reflections contained in these pages are articulated in four parts. Having recognised the rich experiences which consecrated life is experiencing in the Church at the present time, they wished to express their gratitude and their wholehearted esteem *for what consecrated life is and for what it does (Part 1)*. They did not close their eyes to the difficulties, trials and challenges which consecrated persons are experiencing today but looked upon them as *a new opportunity* to rediscover, more profoundly, the meaning and quality of consecrated life *(Part II)*. The most important challenge is that of a *renewed commitment to the spiritual life*, starting afresh from Christ in adhering to the Gospel and living *the spirituality of communion* in a unique way *(Part III)*. Finally, they wanted to *accompany consecrated persons on the streets of the world* where Christ walked and today is present, where the Church proclaims him as Saviour of the world, where the Trinitarian life spreads communion in a renewed mission *(Part IV)*.

7

PART ONE
CONSECRATED LIFE: THE PRESENCE OF THE LOVE OF CHRIST IN THE MIDST OF HUMANITY

5. Considering the presence and many commitments of consecrated men and women in all areas of ecclesial and social life, the members of the Plenary Session wanted to express to them their sincere appreciation, recognition, and solidarity. This is the feeling of the whole Church which the Pope, addressing the Father, the Source of all good, expressed in this way: " We thank you for the gift of consecrated life which seeks you in faith and which through its universal mission invites all people to draw near to you".[17] Through a transformed existence, it participates in the life of the Trinity and confesses it as the love which saves.[18]

Consecrated persons - monks and nuns, contemplatives, religious dedicated to the works of the apostolate, members of Secular Institutes and Societies of Apostolic life, hermits and consecrated virgins - truly deserve the gratitude of the ecclesial community. Their existence witnesses to their love for Christ as they walk the path proposed in the Gospel and with deep joy commit themselves to the same style of life which he chose for himself.[19] This praiseworthy fidelity, while not seeking any other approval than that of the Lord, "also becomes *a living memorial of Jesus' way of living and acting* as the Incarnate Word in relation to the Father and in relation to the brethren".[20]

A Walk in Time

6. It is precisely in the simple day-to-day living that consecrated life progressively matures to become the proclamation of an alternative way of living to that of the world and the dominant culture. Given this style of life and the search for the Absolute, it suggests, as it

---

[17] *Vita Consecrata*, 111.
[18] Cf. *Vita Consecrata*, 16.
[19] Cf. *Lumen Gentium*, 44.
[20] *Vita Consecrata*, 22.

8

were, a spiritual therapy for the evils of our time. Thus, it is a blessing and a reason for hope, in the heart of the Church, for human life and the very life of the Church.[21]

In addition to the active presence of new generations of consecrated persons who bring the presence of Christ to the world and the splendour of the ecclesial charisms to life, the hidden and fruitful presence of consecrated men and women who are experiencing old age, loneliness, illness and suffering is also particularly significant. In addition to the service already rendered and the wisdom which they can share with others, they add their own particular precious contribution by joining themselves in their sufferings to the patient and glorious Christ for his Body, the Church (cf. *Col* 1:24).

7. In recent years consecrated life has undertaken paths of deepening, purification, communion and mission. In the realm of community dynamics, personal relationships have intensified and at the same time intercultural exchanges, recognised as a benefit and stimulus for the institutions themselves, have been strengthened. The praiseworthy effort to find an exercise of authority and obedience which affirms, enlightens, brings together, integrates and reconciles, more closely inspired by the Gospel, is appreciated. In response to the Pope's recommendations, sensitivity to the requests of Bishops is increasing and there is a growing collaboration among Institutes in the areas of formation and the apostolate.

Relationships within the whole Christian community are improving with a mutual and complimentary *interchange of gifts* among the various ecclesial vocations.[22] It is in fact within the local Churches that concrete pastoral plans which respond to Christ's challenges to reach out to people, to mould communities and to have a deep and incisive influence in bringing Gospel values to bear in society and culture can be established.[23]

From simple formal relationships one willingly moves to a communion lived in mutual charismatic enrichment. This effort can

---

[21] Cf. *Vita Consecrata*, 87.
[22] Cf. *Lumen Gentium*, 13; John Paul II, Post-Synodal Apostolic Exhortation *Christifideles Laici*, 30 December 1988, 20; *Vita Consecrata*, 31.
[23] Cf. *Novo Millennio Ineunte*, 29.

be helpful to all God's people, since the spirituality of communion supplies institutional reality with a soul by prompting a trust and openness wholly in accord with the dignity and responsibility of every baptised person.[24]

For the Holiness of the Whole People of God

8. The call to follow Christ with a special consecration is a gift of the Trinity for God's Chosen People. Recognising in Baptism the common sacramental origin, consecrated men and women share a common vocation to holiness and to the apostolate with other members of the faithful. By being signs of this universal vocation they manifest the specific mission of consecrated life.[25]

Consecrated women and men have received a call to a "new and special consecration",[26] for the good of the Church, which impels them to live a life in imitation of Christ, the Virgin, and the Apostles with impassioned love.[27] In our world this lifestyle stresses the urgency of a prophetic witness which entails *"the affirmation of the primacy of God and of eternal life*, as evidenced in the following and imitation of the chaste, poor and obedient Christ, who was completely consecrated to the glory of God and to the love of his brethren".[28]

Consecrated persons extend a persuasive invitation to reflect upon the primacy of grace and to respond to it through a generous spiritual commitment.[29] Despite widespread secularisation, there is a widespread demand for spirituality which is often expressed as a renewed need for prayer.[30] Life's events, even in their ordinariness, present themselves as challenges which should be seen in light of conversion. The dedication of consecrated persons to the service of an evangelical quality of life contributes to *the keeping alive in many ways the spiritual practices among the Christian people.* Religious communities increasingly seek to be places for hearing and sharing

---

[24] Cf. *Novo Millennio Ineunte*, 45.
[25] Cf. *Vita Consecrata*, 32.
[26] *Vita Consecrata*, 31.
[27] Cf. *Vita Consecrata*, 28, 94.
[28] *Vita Consecrata*, 85.
[29] Cf. *Novo Millennio Ineunte*, 38.
[30] Cf. *Novo Millennio Ineunte*, 33.

the Word, for liturgical celebration, for the teaching of prayer, and for accompaniment through spiritual direction. Thus, even without realising it, this help given to others offers mutual advantages.[31]

On Mission for the Kingdom

9. In imitation of Jesus, those whom God calls to follow him are consecrated and invited to continue his mission in the world. Indeed, consecrated life itself, guided by the action of the Holy Spirit, becomes a mission. The more consecrated persons allow themselves to be conformed to Christ, the more Christ is made present and active in history for the salvation of all.[32] Open to the needs of the world as seen through the eyes of God, they point to a future with the hope of resurrection, ready to follow the example of Christ who came among us that we "might have life and have it to the full" (*Jn* 10:10).

Zeal for the establishment of the Kingdom of God and the salvation of brothers and sisters thus constitutes the best proof of a self-offering authentically lived by consecrated persons. That is why every new attempt at renewal can be seen as a new impetus for the evangelising mission.[33] With the help of ongoing formation consecrated persons learn to choose from among intense spiritual experiences which lead to courageous decisions.

The interventions of the members in the Plenary and the reports presented called forth admiration for the varied missionary activity of consecrated persons. In a particular way we recognise the preciousness of apostolic work carried out with generosity and the particular richness of the "feminine genius" of consecrated women. *This merits the greatest recognition on the part of all, of pastors and of the faithful.* But the path embarked upon must be deepened and extended. "It is therefore urgently necessary to take certain concrete steps beginning by *providing room for women to participate* in different fields and at all levels including decision making processes".[34]

---

[31] Cf. *Vita Consecrata*, 103.
[32] Cf. *Vita Consecrata*, 72.
[33] Cf. *Novo Millennio Ineunte*, 2.
[34] *Vita Consecrata*, 58.

A word of thanks is especially extended *to those who find themselves on the front lines.* Availability for the mission is attested to with a courageous outreach to people who are still waiting to hear the first proclamation of the Gospel. Perhaps more than ever before, precisely at a time when some Institutes are experiencing a decrease in numbers, many new foundations have come into being. Looking through the lessons of history for an answer to the hopes of humanity, some Gospel-inspired initiatives and daring have compelled consecrated men and women into difficult positions even to the risk of and the effective sacrificing of life.[35]

While carrying out the Gospel works of mercy with renewed concern, many consecrated persons are encountering sick people to care for and those in every kind of need, afflicted by old and new forms of poverty. They are making crucial contributions in other ministries as well, such as that of education which enables the faith to mature through catechesis or even in exercising a true intellectual apostolate. With sacrifice and greater collaboration they also sustain the voice of the Church in the means of communication which promote social transformation.[36] Deeply convinced of the need, an increased number of men and women religious has chosen to live among those who are excluded. Amidst a humanity in movement, where many are forced to emigrate, these men and women of the Gospel push forward to the *border* for the love of Christ, making the last first.

The highly spiritual contribution which nuns offer to evangelisation is also very significant. It is "the soul and yeast of apostolic activity leaving the active participation in it to those whose vocation it is".[37] "Thus their lives become a mysterious source of apostolic fruitfulness and blessing for the Christian Community and the whole world".[38]

Finally, it is fitting to recall that in recent years the *Martyrology of the witnesses of faith and love in consecrated life* has been further and notably enriched. Difficult situations have required

---

[35] Cf. *Evangelii Nuntiandi*, 69; cf. *Novo Millennio Ineunte*, 7.
[36] Cf. *Vita Consecrata*, 99.
[37] Congregation for Institutes of Consecrated Life and Societies of Apostolic Life, *Verbi Sponsa*, Instruction on the Contemplative Life and the Enclosure of Nuns, Vatican City, 13 May 1999, 7.
[38] *Ibid.*; cf. *Perfectae Caritatis*, 7; cf. *Vita Consecrata*, 8, 59.

from not a few consecrated persons the extreme proof of love in genuine faithfulness to the Kingdom. Consecrated to Christ and to the service of his Kingdom, their witness in following him, has brought them to the point of the cross. Though circumstances might differ and situations might vary the cause of martyrdom is always the same-fidelity to the Lord and to his Gospel: "since it is not the pain which makes the martyr but rather the cause".[39]

Open to the Spirit

10. This is a time when the Spirit is breaking forth, opening up new possibilities. The charismatic dimension of the diverse forms of consecrated life, while always in progress, is never finished. Cooperating with the Spirit, consecrated persons prepare in the Church for the coming of the One who must come, the One who is already the future of humanity in progress. Like Mary, the first consecrated woman, who in virtue of the Holy Spirit and her total self-giving brought Christ into the world to redeem it through a loving self-sacrifice, consecrated persons, remaining open to the Spirit are today called to *stake everything on charity*, "living the commandment of a practical and concrete love for every human being".[40] There is a particular bond of life and dynamism between the Holy Spirit and consecrated life. For this reason, consecrated persons must remain open to the Creator Spirit who works in accord with the Father's will, praising the grace which has been given to them in the beloved Son. This same Spirit radiates the splendour of the mystery on all of existence, spent for the Kingdom of God and the needy and abandoned multitude. The future of consecrated life is therefore entrusted to the dynamism of the author and donor of ecclesial charisms which are placed at the service of the full knowledge and realisation of the Gospel of Jesus Christ.

---

[39] St Augustine, *Sermo* 331, 2: PL 38, 1460.
[40] Cf. *Novo Millennio Ineunte*, 49.

PART TWO
COURAGE TO FACE TRIALS AND CHALLENGES

11. A realistic look at the situation of the Church and of the world impels us to also consider *the difficulties encountered in living consecrated life*. We are all aware of the trials and purification which consecrated life is undergoing in these days. The great treasure of the gift of God is held in fragile earthen vessels (cf. *2 Cor* 4:7) and the mystery of evil also threatens those who dedicate their whole lives to God. In turning our attention now to the sufferings and challenges which trouble consecrated life today, we do so, not to bring a critical judgment or condemnation but to once again show our wholehearted solidarity and loving closeness as those who seek to share not only the joys but also the sufferings. As we consider some particular difficulties, we will seek to do so from the point of view of those who know that the history of the Church is being led by God and that all things work out unto good for those who love him (cf. *Rom* 8:28). With this vision of faith even the negative can be an occasion for a new beginning, if one recognises therein the face of the abandoned and Crucified Christ who took on our limitations even to the point of "bearing our sins in his body on the wood of the cross" (*1 Pt* 2:24).[41] In fact, the grace of God is fully manifested in weakness (cf. *2 Cor* 12:9).

Rediscovering the Meaning and Quality of Consecrated Life

12. The difficulties which consecrated persons face today take on many faces, especially if we take into account the different cultural contexts in which they live.

The decrease in members in many Institutes and their ageing, evident in some parts of the world give rise to the question of whether consecrated life is still a visible witness, capable of attracting young people. If, as is affirmed in some places, the third

---

[41] Cf. *Novo Millennio Ineunte*, 25-26.

millennium will be the time of promotion of the laity, of associations, and of ecclesial movements, we can rightfully ask: what place will be reserved for the traditional forms of consecrated life? Consecrated life, John Paul II reminds us, still has a history to be written together with all the faithful.[42]

We cannot however ignore that, at times, consecrated life has not seemed to have been held in its proper consideration. There have even been times when there was a lack of confidence in it. Given the ongoing religious crisis which heavily confronts parts of our society, consecrated persons, particularly today, are obliged to look for new forms of presence and to raise not a few questions regarding the meaning of their identity and future.

In addition to the life giving thrust, capable of witness and self-sacrifice to the point of martyrdom, consecrated life also experiences the insidiousness of mediocrity in the spiritual life, of the progressive taking on of middle class values and of a consumer mentality. The complex management of works, while required by new social demands and norms of the State, together with the temptations presented by efficiency and activism, run the risk of obscuring Gospel originality and of weakening spiritual motivations. The prevalence of personal projects over community endeavours can deeply corrode the communion of brotherly and sisterly love.

These are real problems which should not be taken lightly. Consecrated persons are not alone in living the tension between secularism and an authentic life of faith, between the fragility of humanity itself and the power of grace; this is the experience of all members of the Church.

13.The difficulties and the questioning which religious life is experiencing today can give rise to a new *kairos*, a time of grace. In these challenges lies hidden an authentic call of the Holy Spirit to rediscover the wealth and potentialities of this form of life.

Having to live in a society where a culture of death often reigns can become a challenge to be stronger witnesses, bearers and servants of life.

---

[42] Cf. *Vita Consecrata*, 110.

The evangelical counsels of chastity, poverty and obedience, lived by Christ in the fullness of his human nature as the Son of God and embraced for the love of God, appear as a way for the full realisation of persons opposed to dehumanisation. They are a powerful antidote to the pollution of spirit, life and culture; they proclaim the liberty of the children of God and the joy of living according to the evangelical beatitudes.

The impression which some have of a decline of appreciation of consecrated life in some sectors of the Church can be seen as an invitation to a liberating purification. Consecrated life does not seek praise and human appreciation, it is repaid by the joy of continuing to work untiringly for the kingdom of God, to be a seed of life which grows in secret, without expecting any reward other than that which the Lord will give in the end (cf. *Mt* 6:6). It finds its identity in the call of the Lord, in following him, in unconditional love and service, which are capable of filling a life to the brim and giving it fulness of meaning.

If in some places consecrated persons become *little flocks* because of a decrease in numbers, this can be seen as a providential sign which invites them to recover their very essential tasks of being leaven, sign and prophecy. The greater the mass of dough to be raised, the greater the quality evangelical leaven called for, and the more exquisite the witness of life and charismatic service of consecrated persons.

The growing awareness of the universality of the call to holiness on the part of all Christians,[43] far from making the belonging to a state of life particularly adapted to the realisation of evangelical perfection superfluous can become an added motive for joy for consecrated persons. They are now closer to the other members of the People of God with whom they share a common path in the following of Christ, in a more authentic communion, in mutual respect, without being superior or inferior. At the same time this awareness challenges them to understand the sign value of consecrated life in relation to the holiness of all the members of the Church.

---

[43] Cf. *Lumen Gentium*, Chapter V.

If in fact it is true that all Christians are called "to the holiness and perfection of their particular state"[44] consecrated persons, thanks to a "new and special consecration"[45] have as their mission that of making Christ's way of life shine through the witness of the evangelical counsels, thereby supporting the faithfulness of the whole body of Christ. This is not a difficulty, it is rather a challenge to originality and to the specific contribution of the charisms of consecrated life, which are at the same time charisms of shared spirituality and of mission which fosters the holiness of the Church.

Clearly these challenges can constitute a powerful call to deepen the living of consecrated life itself whose witness is needed today more than ever. It is fitting to remember the ability of holy foundresses and founders to respond to the challenges and difficulties of their times with a genuine charismatic creativity.

The Task of Superiors

14. In rediscovering the meaning and quality of consecrated life a fundamental task is that of superiors, to whom the service of authority has been entrusted, a demanding and at times disputed task. It requires a constant presence which is able to animate and propose, to recall the *raison d'être* of consecrated life, and to help those entrusted to them to live in a constantly renewed fidelity to the call of the Spirit. A superior cannot renounce the mission of animation, of brotherly/sisterly support, of proposing, of listening and of dialogue. Only in this way can the entire community find itself united in full communion and in apostolic and ministerial service. The directives offered in our Congregation's document *Fraternal Life in Community* remain a topic of great interest, when, in speaking of the aspects of authority which should be evaluated today, recalls the task of spiritual authority, of authority conducive to unity and an authority capable of making final decisions and assuring their implementation.[46]

---

[44] *Lumen Gentium*, 42.
[45] *Vita Consecrata*, 31; cf. *Novo Millennio Ineunte*, 46.
[46] Cf. Congregation for Institutes of Consecrated Life and Societies of Apostolic Life, *Fraternal Life in Community, "Congregavit nos in unum Christi amor"*, Rome, 2 February 1994, 50.

A personal and confident participation in the community's life and mission is required of all its members. Even if, in the end, according to proper law, it is the task of authority to make choices and decisions, daily living in community requires a participation which allows for the exercise of dialogue and discernment. Each individual, then, and the whole community can work out their own life with the plan of God, together carrying out God's will.[47] Coresponsibility and participation are also exercised even in various types of councils at various levels, in order to ensure the constant presence of the Lord who enlightens and guides. The Holy Father did not hesitate to recall *the ancient wisdom* of the monastic tradition for a correct concrete exercise of the spirituality of communion which promotes and assures the effective participation of all.[48]

A serious ongoing formation program, built into a radical reconsideration of the problem of formation in Institutes of Consecrated Life and Societies of Apostolic Life, will help light the way to an authentic path to renewal: renewal in fact "depends primarily upon the formation of their members".[49]

Ongoing Formation

15. The times in which we are living call for a general rethinking of the formation of consecrated men and women, which is no longer limited to one period of life. Not only to enable them to become better able to insert themselves into a reality which changes with a rhythm which is often frenetic but also and more importantly because consecrated life itself, of its nature, calls for the constant openness of those who are called to it. If, in fact, consecrated life is in itself "a progressive taking on of the attitude of Christ",[50] it seems evident that such a path must endure for a lifetime and involve the *whole* person, heart, mind and strength (cf. *Mt* 22:37) reshaping the person in the likeness of the Son who gives himself to the Father for the good of

---

[47] Cf. *Vita Consecrata*, 92.
[48] Cf. *Novo Millennio Ineunte*, 45.
[49] Cf. Congregation for Institutes of Consecrated Life and Societies of Apostolic Life, *Directives on Formation in Religious Institutes, Potissimum Institutioni*, Rome, 2 February 1990, 1.
[50] *Vita Consecrata*, 65.

humanity. Thus understood, formation is no longer only a teaching period in preparation for vows but also represents a *theological* way of thinking of consecrated life which is in itself a never ending formation "sharing in the work of the Father who, through the Spirit, fashions in the heart the inner attitudes of the Son".[51]

Thus it will be important that all consecrated persons be formed in the freedom to learn throughout life, in every age and season, in every human ambient and context, from every person and every culture open to be taught by any fragment of truth and beauty found around them. But above all they must learn to be formed by everyday life, by their own community, by their brothers and sisters, by everyday things, ordinary and extraordinary, by prayer and by apostolic fatigue, in joy and in suffering, until the moment of death.

Openness to the other and to otherness, particularly *a relation with time* become most important. People in ongoing formation take advantage of time, they don't submit to it. They accept it as a gift and wisely enter into the various rhythms of life itself (days, weeks, months, years) with wisdom, seeking the harmony between them and the rhythm, fixed by an immutable and eternal God which marks the *days, centuries and times*. In a very unique way consecrated persons learn to allow themselves to be moulded by *the liturgical year* in which the mysteries of the life of the Son of God are relived in order to start afresh from Christ and from his death and resurrection everyday of their lives.

Vocation Animation

16. One of the first fruits of a path of ongoing formation is the daily ability to live one's vocation as a gift which is always new and to be accepted with a grateful heart: a gift which calls for an ever more responsible attitude, to be witnessed to with an ongoing conviction and attractiveness so that others might feel called to God either in this particular vocation or through other paths. The consecrated person is, by nature, also a vocation animator: one who is called

---

[51] *Vita Consecrata*, 66.

cannot not become a caller. There is, therefore, a natural link between ongoing formation and vocation animation.

Service to vocations is one of the most demanding challenges which consecrated life must face today. On the one hand, the globalisation of culture and the complexity of social relations make radical and lifelong choices difficult; on the other hand, the world is living through a growing experience of moral and material sufferings which undermine the very dignity of the human being and is silently calling for persons who will powerfully announce a message of peace and hope, persons who will bring the salvation of Christ. We are reminded of the words of Jesus: "The harvest is great but the labourers are few. Pray the master of the harvest to send labourers into his harvest" (*Lk* 10:2; *Mt* 9:37-38).

The first task of any vocational pastoral program is always prayer. Especially in those places where few are choosing to enter into consecrated life, a renewed faith in God who can raise Children of Abraham even from stone (cf. *Mt* 3:9) and make sterile wombs fruitful if called upon in faith, is urgently needed. All the faithful, and especially youth, should be involved in this manifestation of faith in God who alone can call and send workers. The entire local Church - bishops, priests, laity, consecrated persons - is called to assume responsibility for vocations to this particular consecration.

The master plan of vocational promotion to consecrated life is that which the Lord himself began when he said to the apostles John and Andrew, *"Come and see"* (*Jn* 1:39). This encounter accompanied by the sharing of life requires that consecrated persons deeply live their consecration in order to become a visible sign of the joy which God gives to those who listen to his call. For this reason, there is a need for communities which are welcoming and able to share the ideal of their life with young people, allowing themselves to be challenged by the demands of authenticity, and willing to accept them.

The local Church is the privileged place for this vocational announcement. Here all the ministries and charisms express their complimentarity.[52] Together they realise communion in the one Spirit of Christ in the many ways that it is manifested. The active

---

[52] Cf. *Christifideles Laici*, 55.

presence of consecrated persons will help Christian communities to become *laboratories of faith,*[53] places of research, of reflection and of meeting, of communion and apostolic service, in which all feel part of the building up of the Kingdom of God. In this way the characteristic climate of the church as God's family, an environment which facilitates mutual knowledge, sharing and the *contagion* of those very values which are at the origin of the choice to give one's whole life to the cause of the Kingdom, is created.

17. Care for vocations is a crucial task for the future of consecrated life. The decrease in vocations particularly in the Western world and their growth in Asia and Africa are drawing a new geography of the presence of consecrated life in the Church and new cultural balances in the lives of Institutes. This state of life which, through the profession of the evangelical counsels gives a constant visibility to the characteristic features of Jesus in the midst of the world,[54] is today undergoing a particular period of rethinking and of research with new methods in new cultures. This is certainly a promising beginning for the development of unexplored expressions of its multiple charismatic forms.

The transformations which are taking place directly involve each Institute of Consecrated Life and Society of Apostolic Life, calling them to give strong Gospel-based meaning to their presence in the Church and their service to humanity. Vocational ministry requires the development of new and deeper means of encounter; of offering a living witness of the characteristics of the following of Christ and of holiness, of presenting ways which strongly and clearly announce the freedom which springs from a life of poverty whose only treasure is the kingdom of God, the depths of love of a chaste existence which seeks only one heart, that of Christ, and the strength for sanctification and renewal contained in an obedient life whose only goal is to carry out the will of God for the salvation of the world.

Today vocation promotion is not something which can be delegated in an exclusive way to some specialists dedicated to the task, nor can

---

[53] Cf. John Paul II, *Homily at the Vigil of Torvergata* (20 August 2000): *L'Osservatore Romano,* 21-22 August 2000, n.3, p.4.
[54] Cf. *Vita Consecrata,* 1.

it be separated from a true, specific youth ministry which first and foremost communicates Christ's love for youth. Every community and all the members of the Institute are called to take on the tasks of contact with youth, of an evangelical teaching of the following of Christ and of handing on the charism. Young people are searching for others who are able to propose styles of authentic evangelical life and ways of arriving at the great spiritual values of human and Christian life. Consecrated persons must rediscover the teaching art of bringing to the surface and freeing the deep questions which are too often kept hidden in one's heart. This is especially true when dealing with young people. As they accompany others on the path of vocational discernment, consecrated persons will be forced to share the source of their identity. Communicating one's own life experience always entails remembering and revisiting that light which guided the person to his or her own particular vocational choice.

The Formative Courses

18. As far as formation is concerned, our Dicastery has issued two documents, *Potissimum Institutioni,* and *Inter-Institute Collaboration for Formation.* However, we are well aware of the constant challenges which Institutes must face in this field.

The new vocations knocking at the doors of consecrated life present great diversity and require personal attention and methods which are able to respond to their concrete human, spiritual and cultural situations. For this reason, a peaceful discernment, freed from the temptations of numbers or efficiency, must take place in order to verify the authenticity of the vocation and the purity of motivation in the light of faith and of possible contradictions. Young people need to be challenged to meet the high ideals of a radical following of Christ and the profound demands of holiness, when discerning a vocation which is beyond them and which perhaps goes beyond the initial ideas which attracted them to enter a particular Institute. For this reason, formation must have the characteristics of the *initiation to the radical following of Christ.* "Since the very purpose of consecrated life is conformity to the

Lord Jesus" it is necessary to begin "a path of gradual identification with the attitude of Christ towards the Father".[55] This will help to integrate theological, humanistic and technical studies with the spiritual and apostolic life of the Institute and will always conserve the characteristic of a "school of holiness".

The most pressing challenges which formation must face grow out of the values of today's globalised culture. The Christian announcement of life as vocation, that is, one which flows from God's loving plan and requires a personal and salvific encounter with Christ in the Church must confront the dominant ideals and plans of cultures and social histories which are extremely diversified. There is the risk that subjective choices, individual projects and local customs will prevail over the rule, the style of community life and the apostolic projects of the community. This calls for a formative dialogue capable of bringing together the human, social and spiritual characteristics borne by each person, discerning in them the human limitations which must be overcome and the promptings of the Spirit which can renew the lives of individuals and Institutes. In a period of profound changes, formation must be attentive to the need to plant in the hearts of young consecrated persons those human, spiritual and charismatic values necessary to make them suitable to carry out a "creative fidelity"[56] in the paths of the spiritual and apostolic tradition of the Institute.

Institutes of Consecrated Life are increasingly characterised by cultural, age and project differences. Formation should prepare for community dialogue in the cordiality and charity of Christ, teaching to see diversity as richness and to integrate the various ways of seeing and feeling. Thus the constant search for unity in charity will become a *school of communion* for Christian communities and an example of people living together in communion.

Particular attention must be given to a cultural formation in line with the times and in dialogue with the research of the meaning of human life today. This calls for a greater preparation in the philosophical, theological and psychological fields and a more profound orientation to the spiritual life, models more adapted to

---

[55] Cf. *Vita Consecrata*, 65.
[56] *Vita Consecrata*, 37.

the cultures in which new vocations are being born and well-planned programs for ongoing formation. Above all it is hoped that the best forces are destined for formation even when this calls for great sacrifices. The use of qualified personnel and their adequate preparation must be a priority commitment.

We must be very generous in dedicating our time and best energies to formation. The consecrated persons themselves are, in fact, the best resources that we have. Without them all formative and apostolic plans remain theory and useless desires. In an era as rushed as ours, perseverance and patient waiting to realise the scope of formation are called for more than ever. In circumstances in which rapidity and superficiality prevail we need serenity and depth because, in reality, a person is fashioned very slowly.

Some Particular Challenges

19. Importance has been placed on the quality of life and the demands of formation because these seem to be the areas which are in most need of attention. The Congregation for Institutes of Consecrated Life and Societies of Apostolic Life wishes to be close to consecrated persons in all problem areas and to continue an ever more sincere and constructive dialogue. The members of the Plenary are aware of this need and have manifested the desire for a greater knowledge of and collaboration with Institutes of Consecrated Life and Societies of Apostolic Life. Their presence in the local Church and particularly that of congregations of diocesan right, consecrated virgins and hermits require special attention on the part of the Bishops and their presbyterates.

In the same way they are aware of the questions posed by religious regarding the great works in which up to now they have been allowed to serve in line with their respective charisms: hospitals, schools, houses of welcome and of retreat. In some parts of the world these are urgently needed, in other parts they are becoming difficult to administer. Creativity, wisdom and dialogue among members of the Institute, among Institutes with similar works and with those responsible for the local Church are necessary in order to find the right answers.

The themes of inculturation are also very much alive. These deal with the way in which to incarnate consecrated life, adaptation of forms of spirituality and apostolate, ways of governing, formation, use of resources and material goods and the carrying out of mission. The appeals expressed by the Pope regarding the whole Church are also applicable to consecrated life. "In the third millennium, Christianity will have to respond ever more effectively to this *need for inculturation*. Christianity, while remaining completely true to itself, with unswerving faith to the proclamation of the Gospel and the tradition of the Church, will also reflect the different faces of the cultures and peoples in which it is received and takes root".[57] A true inculturation in consecrated life and in the whole Church will result in a notable enrichment and a new season of spiritual and apostolic growth.

We could endlessly list other expectations of consecrated life at the beginning of this new millennium because the Spirit always pushes us above and beyond. It is the word of the Teacher who, with great enthusiasm, must provoke all of the disciples to remember the past with gratitude, to live the present with enthusiasm and to look forward to the future in confidence.[58]

Listening to the invitation given to the whole Church by John Paul II, consecrated life must clearly start afresh from Christ, contemplating his face, giving preference to the ways of spirituality as life, teaching and pastoral practice. "The Church also awaits your contribution, Consecrated Brothers and Sisters, to advance this new track of street according to the paths which I outlined in the Apostolic Letter *Novo millennio ineunte: contemplate* the face of Christ, *start afresh* from Him, *witness* to His love".[59] Only then will consecrated life find new vitality to place itself at the service of the whole Church and all of humanity.

---

[57] *Novo Millennio Ineunte*, 40.
[58] Cf. *Novo Millennio Ineunte*, 1.
[59] John Paul II, *Homily* (2 February 2001): *L'Osservatore Romano*, 4 February 2001, p.4.

PART THREE
SPIRITUAL LIFE IN THE FIRST PLACE

20. Consecrated Life, like all forms of Christian life, is by its nature dynamic and all who are called by the Spirit to embrace it must constantly renew themselves in growing towards that perfect stature of the Body of Christ (cf. *Eph* 4:13). It came into being through the creative prompting of the Spirit who moved founders and foundresses along the Gospel path, giving rise to an admirable variety of charisms. These founders and foundresses, open and docile to the Spirit's guidance, followed Christ more closely, entered into intimacy with him and fully shared in his mission.

Their experience of the Spirit must not only be preserved by those who follow them but must also be deepened and developed.[60] Today, too, an openness and docility to the Spirit's action which is always new and creative is required. The Spirit alone can keep alive the freshness and authenticity of the beginnings while at the same time instilling the courage of interdependence and inventiveness needed to respond to the signs of the times.

We must therefore allow ourselves to be led by the Spirit to a constantly renewed discovery of God and of his Word, to a burning love for God and for humanity and to a new understanding of the charism which has been given. It calls for a concentration on an intense spirituality in the strongest sense of the word, that is, *life according to the Spirit*. Consecrated life today needs a spiritual rebirth which will help to concretely bring about the spiritual and evangelical meaning of baptismal consecration and of its *new and special consecration*.

"The spiritual life must therefore have first place in the programme of Families of consecrated life, in such a way that every Institute and community will be a school of true evangelical spirituality".[61] We must allow the Spirit to superabundantly break

---

[60] Cf. *Mutuae Relationes*, 11; *Vita Consecrata*, 37
[61] *Vita Consecrata*, 93.

open the streams of living water which flow from Christ. It is the Spirit who allows us to recognise the Lord in Jesus of Nazareth (cf. *1 Cor* 12:3) who makes us hear the call to follow him and who unifies us in him. Anyone who does not have the Spirit of Christ, does not belong to Christ (cf. *Rom* 8:9). It is the Spirit who, making us sons and daughters in the Son, gives witness to the paternity of God, makes us aware of our status as sons and daughters and gives us the courage to dare to call him "Abba, Father" (*Rom* 8:15). It is the Spirit who instills love and gives birth to communion. Clearly consecrated life needs a renewed striving for holiness which in the simplicity of everyday life, aims at the radicalness of the Sermon on the Mount[62] and demanding love, lived in a personal relationship with the Lord, in a life of communion and in the service to every man and woman. It is such an interior newness, entirely animated by the strength of the Spirit and reaching out to the Father, seeking the Kingdom, which will allow consecrated persons to *start afresh from Christ* and be witnesses of his love.

The call to return to one's own roots and choices in spirituality opens paths to the future. First of all it requires living the fullness of the theology of the evangelical counsels with the model of Trinitarian life as the starting point, according to the teachings of *Vita Consecrata*,[63] with a new opportunity to come into contact with the sources of one's own charism and constitutional texts, which are always open to new and more demanding interpretations. This dynamic sense of spirituality provides the opportunity to develop, at this stage of the Church's history, a deeper spirituality which is more ecclesial and communitarian, more demanding and mature in mutual support in striving for holiness, more generous in apostolic choices; finally, a spirituality which is more open to becoming a *teaching and pastoral plan for holiness* within consecrated life itself and in its radiance for the entire people of God. The Holy Spirit is the soul and animator of Christian spirituality; for this reason we must entrust ourselves to the Spirit's action which departs from the intimacy of hearts, manifests itself in communion and spreads itself in mission.

---

[62] Cf. *Novo Millennio Ineunte*, 31.
[63] Cf. *Vita Consecrata*, 20-21.

Starting Afresh from Christ

21. Therefore it is necessary to adhere ever more closely to Christ, the centre of consecrated life and once again take up the path of conversion and renewal which, like the initial experience of the apostles, before and after the resurrection, was a *starting afresh from Christ.* Yes, one must start afresh from Christ because it was from him that the first disciples started in Galilee; from him, that throughout history men and women of every status and culture, consecrated by the Spirit in the strength of their call, have started out; for him they have left family and homeland, following him unconditionally, making themselves available for the announcement of the Kingdom and doing good for all (cf. *Acts* 10:38).

The awareness of one's own poverty and fragility and the greatness of the call have often resulted in the repetition of the words of the apostle Peter, "Leave me Lord, I am a sinful man" (Lk 5:8). And yet God's gift was stronger than human weakness. In fact, it is Christ who has made himself present in the communities of those who throughout the centuries have gathered in his name, he taught them about himself and about his Spirit, he oriented them towards the Father, he guided them along the streets of the world to encounter brothers and sisters, he made them instruments of his love and builders of his Kingdom in communion with all the other vocations in the Church.

Consecrated persons can and must start afresh from Christ because he himself first came to them and accompanied them on the path (cf. *Lk* 24:13-22). Their life is the proclamation of the primacy of grace.[64] Without Christ they can do nothing (cf. *Jn* 15:5); however, in him who gives strength they can do all (cf. *Phil* 4:13).

22. *Staring afresh from Christ* means proclaiming that consecrated life is a special following of Christ, "*a living memorial of Jesus' way of living and acting* as the Incarnate Word in relation to the Father and in relation to the brethren".[65] This implies a particular communion of love for Christ who has become the centre of their life and the continual source of every initiative. It is, as the

---

[64] Cf. *Novo Millennio Ineunte*, 38.
[65] *Vita Consecrata*, 22.

Apostolic Exhortation *Vita Consecrata* reminds us, an experience of sharing, "a special grace of intimacy".[66] It is "becoming one with him, taking on his mind and his way of life",[67] and it is a life "taken up by Christ",[68] "touched by the hand of Christ, a life where his voice is heard, a life sustained by his grace".[69]

The whole life of consecration can be summarised by this point of departure alone: *the evangelical counsels* make sense only in as much as they help to safeguard and foster love for the Lord in full openness to his will; *Community life* is motivated by the One who gathers others around himself and has as its goal the enjoyment of his constant presence; *the mission* is his command leading us to seek his face in the faces of those to whom we are sent to share with them the experience of Christ.

These were the intentions of the founders and foundresses of different communities and Institutes of Consecrated Life. These are the ideals which have motivated generations of consecrated women and men.

Starting afresh from Christ means once again finding one's first love, the inspiring spark which first gave rise to the following. The primacy of love is his. The following is only a response in love to the love of God. If "we love" it is "because he first loved us"(*1 Jn* 4:10, 19). This means recognising his personal love with that heartfelt awareness which made the apostle Paul say: "Christ loved *me* and gave up his life for *me*" (*Gal* 2:20).

Only the awareness of being infinitely loved can help us overcome every personal and institutional difficulty. Consecrated persons cannot be creative, capable of renewing the Institute and opening new pastoral paths if they do not feel loved with this love. It is this love which makes them strong and courageous which instills fire and enables them to dare all.

The vows with which one commits oneself to live the evangelical counsels confer their radicalness as a response to love. Virginity opens the heart to the measure of Christ's heart and makes it

---

[66] *Vita Consecrata*, 16.
[67] *Vita Consecrata*, 18.
[68] *Vita Consecrata*, 25.
[69] *Vita Consecrata*, 40.

possible to love as he loved. Poverty frees one from the slavery to things and to artificial needs which drive consumer society and leads to the rediscovery of Christ, the only treasure truly worth living for. Obedience places life entirely in Christ's hands so that he may use it according to God's design and make it a masterpiece. Courage is needed for a generous and joyous following.

Contemplating the Faces of Christ

23. The path which consecrated life is called to take up at the beginning of the new millennium is guided by the contemplation of Christ with a gaze *fixed, more than ever, on the face of the Lord.*[70] But where does one concretely contemplate the face of Christ? There are a multiplicity of presences to be discovered in ways that are ever new.

Christ is truly present in his Word and in the Sacraments, especially in the Eucharist. Christ lives in the Church, he makes himself present in the community of those who are gathered in his name. He is before us in every person, identifying himself in a special way with the small, the poor, those who suffer and those most in need. He meets us in every event happy or sad, in trials and in joys, in pain and in sickness.

Holiness is the fruit of the encounter with him in the many presences in which we can discover his face as the Son of God, a suffering face and at the same time the face of the Risen One. As he once made himself present in daily life he is still present in daily life today where he continues to show his face. Recognising him requires a gaze of faith which is acquired through the habitual reading of the Word of God, through prayer and above all through the exercise of charity because the Mystery can only be fully known through love.

We can recall some privileged *places* in which the face of Christ can be contemplated, *for a renewed commitment in the life of the Spirit.* These are walking the paths of a lived spirituality, a priority commitment in this time, taking the opportunity to re-read in life and in daily experiences the spiritual riches of one's own charism, through of a renewed contact with the same sources which, inspired

---

[70] *Novo Millennio Ineunte,* 16.

by the founders' and foundress' experience of the Spirit, gave rise to the spark of new life and new works, the specific re-reading of the Gospel found in every Charism.

The Word of God

24. John Paul II reminds consecrated persons that living spirituality means first of all starting afresh from the person of Christ, true God and true man, present in his Word, "the first source of all spirituality".[71] Holiness is inconceivable without a renewed listening to the word of God. In *Novo Millennio Ineunte*, we read: "It is especially necessary that listening to the Word of God should become a life giving encounter... which draws from the biblical text the living Word which questions, directs and shapes our lives".[72] It is there, in fact, where the Master reveals himself and educates the mind and the heart: It is there that the vision of faith matures, learning to look at reality and events through the eyes of God, to the point of having "the mind of Christ" (*1 Cor* 2:16).

It was the Holy Spirit who sparked the Word of God with new light for the founders and foundresses. Every charism and every Rule springs from it and seeks to be an expression of it. In continuity with founders and foundresses their disciples today are called to take up the Word of God and to cherish it in their hearts so that it may be a lamp for their feet and a light for their path (cf. *Ps* 118:105). The Holy Spirit will then be able to lead them to the fullness of truth (cf. *Jn* 16:13).

The Word of God is nourishment for life, for prayer and for the daily journey, the principle which unifies the community in oneness of thought, the inspiration for ongoing renewal and apostolic creativity. The Second Vatican Council had already indicated that the first great principle of renewal is a return to the Gospel.[73]

Within communities and in groups of consecrated men and women, as in the whole Church, a more lively and immediate contact with the Word of God has developed in recent years. It is a

---

[71] *Vita Consecrata*, 94.
[72] *Novo Millennio Ineunte*, 39.
[73] Cf. *Perfectae Caritatis*, 2.

path which must continue to be walked down with an ever greater intensity. The Pope has said: "You must not tire of meditating on *Holy Scripture* and above all on the *Gospels* so that they can imprint upon you the features of the Incarnate Word".[74]

Community life also fosters the rediscovery of the ecclesial dimension of the Word: receive it, meditate upon it, live it together, communicate the experiences which blossom from it and thus submit yourself to an authentic spirituality of communion.

In this context it is good to remember the need for constant reference to the Rule, because in the Rule and in the Constitutions "there is a map for the whole journey of discipleship in accordance with a specific charism confirmed by the Church".[75] This way of following translates the particular interpretation of the Gospel given by the founders and foundresses as the result of a particular prompting of the Spirit and it helps the members of the Institute live concretely according to the Word of God.

Nourished by the word, made new, free and conformed to the Gospels, consecrated men and women can be authentic *servants of the Word* in the task of evangelisation. This is how they carry out a priority for the Church at the beginning of the new millennium: "we must rekindle in ourselves the impetus of the beginnings and allow ourselves to be filled with the ardour of the apostolic preaching which followed Pentecost".[76]

Prayer and Contemplation

25. Prayer and contemplation provide the ambient for the reception of the Word of God and at the same time they spring from listening to the Word. Without an interior life of love which draws the Word, the Father and the Spirit to itself, an outlook of faith is impossible (cf. *Jn* 14:23). As a consequence life itself loses meaning, the faces of brothers and sisters are obscured and it becomes impossible to recognise the face of God in them, historical events remain ambiguous and deprived of hope and

---

[74] John Paul II, *Homily* (2 February 2001): *L'Osservatore Romano*, 4 February 2001.
[75] *Vita Consecrata*, 37.
[76] *Novo Millennio Ineunte*, 40.

apostolic and charitable mission become nothing more than widespread activity.

Every vocation to consecrated life is born in contemplation, from moments of intense communion and from a deep relationship of friendship with Christ, from the beauty and light which was seen shining on his face. From there the desire to always be with the Lord-and to follow him-matures:"how good it is for us to be here" (*Mt* 17:4). Every vocation must constantly mature in this intimacy with Christ. "Your first task therefore" -John Paul reminds consecrated persons- "cannot not be in the line of *contemplation*. Every reality of consecrated life is born and is regenerated each day in the unending contemplation of the face of Christ".[77]

Monks and cloistered nuns like hermits dedicate more time to praise of God as well as to prolonged silent prayer. Members of Secular Institutes, like consecrated virgins in the world, offer to God the joys and sorrows, the hopes and petitions of all people and contemplate the face of Christ which they recognise in the faces of their brothers and sisters, in the historical events, in the apostolate and in everyday work. Religious men and women dedicated to teaching, to the care of the sick, to the poor, encounter the face of the Lord there. For missionaries and members of Societies of Apostolic Life the proclamation of the Gospel is lived according to the example of St Paul, as authentic cult (cf. *Rom* 1:6). The whole Church enjoys and benefits from the many forms of prayer and the variety of ways in which the one face of Christ is contemplated.

At the same time it is noticeable that, for many years now, the liturgical prayer of the Hours and the celebration of the Eucharist have assumed a central position in the life of all types of communities and of fraternities, once again giving them a biblical and ecclesial vigour. They also foster mutual edification and can become a witness to be before God and with God, *"a house and a school of communion"*.[78] An authentic spiritual life requires that everyone, in all the diverse vocations, regularly dedicate, every day, appropriate times to enter deeply into silent conversation with him

---

[77] John Paul II, *Homily* (2 February 2001): *L'Osservatore Romano*, 4 February 2001.
[78] *Novo Millennio Ineunte*, 43.

by whom they know they are loved, to share their very lives with him and to receive enlightenment to continue on the daily journey. It is an exercise which requires fidelity, because we are constantly being bombarded by the estrangements and excesses which come from today's society, especially from the means of communication. At times fidelity to personal and liturgical prayer will require a true effort not to allow oneself to be swallowed up in frenetic activism. Otherwise it will be impossible to bear fruit. "No more than a branch can bear fruit of itself apart from the vine can you bear fruit apart from me" (*Jn* 15:4).

The Eucharist, a Privileged Place
for Encounter with the Lord

26. Giving a priority place to spirituality means starting afresh from the rediscovered *centrality of the Eucharistic celebration*, a privileged place of encounter with the Lord. There he once again makes himself present in the midst of the disciples, he explains the Scriptures, he warms the heart and enlightens the mind, he opens eyes and allows himself to be recognised (cf. *Lk* 24:13-35). John Paul II's invitation extended to consecrated persons is particularly vibrant: "My dearest ones, encounter him and contemplate him in a very special way in the Eucharist, celebrated and adored every day as source and summit of existence and apostolic action".[79] In the Apostolic Exhortation *Vita Consecrata* he called for participation in the Sacrament of the Eucharist and assiduous and prolonged Eucharistic adoration daily.[80] The Eucharist, the memorial of the Lord's sacrifice, the heart of the life of the Church and of every community, fashions from within the renewed offering of one's very existence, the project of community life and the apostolic mission. We all need the daily *viaticum* of encounter with the Lord in order to bring every day life into sacred time which is made present in celebration of the Lord's Memorial.

Here the fulness of *intimacy* with Christ is realised, *becoming one*

---

[79] John Paul II, *Homily* (2 February 2001): *L'Osservatore Romano*, 4 February 2001.
[80] *Vita Consecrata*, 95.

with him, total conformity to him to whom consecrated persons are called by vocation.[81] In fact, in the Eucharist, Jesus joins us to himself in his very paschal offering to the Father. We offer and are offered. Religious consecration itself assumes a Eucharistic structure, it is the total offering of self closely joined to the Eucharistic Sacrifice.

In the Eucharist all forms of prayer come together, the Word of God is proclaimed and received, relationships with God, with brothers and sisters, with all men and women are challenged. It is the Sacrament of filiation, of communion and of mission. The Eucharist, the Sacrament of unity with Christ, is at the same time the Sacrament of Church unity and community unity for the consecrated person. Clearly it is "The source of spirituality both for individuals and for communities".[82]

In order to fully produce the expected fruits of communion and renewal, the essential conditions must be present, especially mutual forgiveness and the commitment to love one another in accord with the Lord's teaching; full reconciliation is necessary before presenting ones's offering at the altar (cf. *Mt* 5:23). The Sacrament of unity cannot be celebrated while remaining indifferent to others. On the other hand, it must be remembered that these *essential conditions* are also *the fruit and sign* of a well-celebrated Eucharist because it is especially in communion with the Eucharistic Jesus that we are enabled to love and to forgive. Moreover, every celebration should become the occasion to renew the commitment of giving one's life for others in acceptance and in service. Thus, Christ's promise, "Where two or three are gathered in my name, there am I in their midst" (*Mt* 18:20), would hold true, in the fullest sense, for the Eucharistic celebration, and gathered around the Eucharist, the community will be renewed daily.

Meeting these conditions the community of consecrated persons which lives the Paschal Mystery, renewed daily in the Eucharist, becomes a witness of communion and a prophetic sign of solidarity for a divided and wounded society. In fact, the spirituality of communion, so necessary to establish the dialogue of charity needed in today's world, is born in the Eucharist.[83]

---

[81] Cf. *Vita Consecrata*, 18.
[82] *Vita Consecrata*, 95.
[83] Cf. *Vita Consecrata*, 51.

The Face of Christ in Trials

27. Living spirituality in a continual *starting afresh from Christ* means always starting from the greatest expression of his love-and the Eucharist relives the mystery of this moment-when on the cross Jesus gives his very life as the greatest gift of self. Those who have been called to live the evangelical counsels through profession must frequently contemplate the face of the Crucified One.[84] He is the source from whom we learn what love is and how God and humanity should be loved, the source of all charisms, the summary of all vocations.[85] Consecration, a total sacrifice and perfect holocaust, is the way suggested to them by the Spirit to relive the mystery of the Crucified Christ, who came into the world to give his life as a ransom for many (cf. *Mt* 20:28; *Mk* 10:45) and to respond to his infinite love.

The history of consecrated life has expressed this configuration to Christ in many ascetic forms which "have constituted and continue to constitute an authentic path to holiness. Asceticism... is truly indispensable if consecrated persons are to remain faithful to their own vocation and follow Jesus on the way of the cross".[86] Today, consecrated persons, while maintaining the experience of the centuries, are called to find forms which are consonant with our times. Forms which assure a generosity of service and support the fatigue of apostolic work. Today, the cross which they take up daily (cf. *Lk* 9:23), such as the age of the Institute, structural inadequacy, and uncertainty regarding the future, can also take on collective value.

In the face of so many personal, communal and social sufferings one can hear the cry of Christ on the cross, "Why have you abandoned me?" (*Mk* 15:34), reechoed in the hearts of individuals or of whole communities. In that cry, addressed to the Father, Jesus makes us understand that his solidarity with humanity was so radical that it penetrated, shared and assumed every negative aspect even to death, the fruit of sin. "In order to bring men back to the

---

[84] Cf. *Novo Millennio Ineunte*, 25-27.
[85] Cf. *Vita Consecrata*, 23.
[86] *Vita Consecrata*, 38.

Father's face, Jesus not only had to take on the face of man, but he had to burden himself with the 'face' of sin".[87]

Starting afresh from Christ means recognising that sin is still radically present in the heart and life of all, and discovering in the suffering face of Christ that offering which reconciled humanity with God.

Throughout the history of the Church, consecrated women and men have contemplated the *suffering face* even outside themselves. They recognised it in the sick, the imprisoned, the poor and the sinner. Their battle was primarily against sin and its fatal consequences: Jesus' proclamation "Convert and believe the Good News" (*Mk* 1:15) moved them to reach out to others and provided the hope of new life where discouragement and death reigned. Their service has brought many men and women to experience the merciful embrace of God the Father in the Sacrament of Penance. Today too, there is a need to strongly repropose this *ministry of reconciliation* (cf. *2 Cor* 5:18) entrusted by Jesus Christ to the Church. This is the *mysterium pietatis*[88] which consecrated men and women are called to experience frequently in the Sacrament of Penance.

Today new faces are appearing in which to recognise, love and serve the face of Christ where he has made himself present; *they are the new material moral and spiritual poverties* produced by contemporary society. The cry of Jesus on the cross reveals how he took all this evil upon himself in order to redeem it. The vocation of consecrated persons continues to be that of Jesus and like him they take upon themselves the pain and the sin of the world, consuming them in love.

The Spirituality of Communion

28. If *"the spiritual life must have first place in the program of the Families of consecrated life"*[89] it should be above all a spirituality of communion suitable for the present time. "To make the Church the home and school of communion: that is the great challenge facing us in the millennium which is now beginning, if we wish to

---

[87] *Novo Millennio Ineunte*, 25.
[88] Cf. *Novo Millennio Ineunte*, 37.
[89] *Vita Consecrata*, 93.

be faithful to God's plan and respond to the world's deepest yearnings".[90]

The whole Church expects a clear contribution to this undertaking from consecrated life because of its specific vocation to a life of communion in love. In *Vita Consecrata* we read "*Consecrated Persons* are asked to be true experts of communion and to practice its spirituality as witnesses and artisans of that plan of communion which stands at the center of history according to God".[91]

Moreover, we are reminded that one of the tasks of consecrated life today is that of *spreading the spirituality of communion*, first of all in their internal life and then in the Church community, and even beyond its boundaries, by beginning or continuing a dialogue in charity, especially in those places where today's world is torn apart by ethnic hatred or senseless violence".[92] This is a task which requires spiritual persons interiorly shaped by God, by loving and merciful communion and by mature communities where the spirituality of communion is the rule of life.

29. But what is the spirituality of communion? With incisive words, capable of giving new life to relationships and programs, John Paul II teaches: "A spirituality of communion indicates above all the heart's contemplation of the mystery of the Trinity dwelling within us and whose light we must also be able to see shining on the faces of the brothers and sisters around us. A spirituality of communion also means an ability to think of our brothers and sisters in faith within the profound unity of the Mystical Body and therefore as 'those who are part of me'...". Some consequences of *feeling* and *doing* derive from this principal with convincing logic: sharing the joys and sufferings of our brothers and sisters; sensing their desires and attending to their needs; offering them true and profound friendship. The spirituality of communion also implies the ability to see what is positive in others, to welcome it and to prize it as a gift from God, and to know how to make room for others, sharing each other's

---

[90] *Novo Millennio Ineunte*, 43.
[91] *Vita Consecrata*, 46.
[92] *Vita Consecrata*, 51.

burdens. Unless we follow this spiritual path, the external structures of communion serve very little purpose.[93]

The spirituality of communion which appears to reflect the spiritual climate of the Church at the beginning of the third millennium is an active and exemplary task for consecrated life on all levels. It is the principle highway for the future of life and witness. Holiness and mission come through the community because in and through it Christ makes himself present. Brother and sister become Sacraments of Christ and of the encounter with God, the concrete possibility, and even more, the unsurpassable necessity in carrying out the commandment to love one another and bring about Trinitarian communion.

In recent years communities and various types of fraternities of consecrated persons are seen as places of communion where relationships seem to be less formal and where acceptance and mutual understanding are facilitated. The divine and human value of being together freely in friendship and sharing even moments of relaxation and recreation together as disciples gathered around Christ the Teacher is being rediscovered.

Moreover there is a more intense communion among the different communities of the same Institute: multi-cultural and International communities, called to "witness to the sense of communion among peoples, races, and cultures",[94] are already in many areas a positive reality where mutual knowledge, respect, esteem and enrichment are being experienced. They prove to be training grounds for integration and inculturation and at the same time a witness to the universality of the Christian message.

The Exhortation *Vita Consecrata*, presenting this form of life as *a sign of communion in the Church*, emphasised all the wealth and demands expected of community life. Earlier our Dicastery had promulgated the document *Congregavit nos in unum Christi amor*, on community life. Every community should periodically go back to these documents to evaluate its own journey of faith and progress in communion.

---

[93] Cf. *Novo Millennio Ineunte*, 43.
[94] *Vita Consecrata*, 51.

Communion between Old and New Charisms

30. The communion which consecrated persons are called to live goes far beyond their own religious family or Institute. Opening themselves to communion with other Institutes and other forms of consecration, they can spread communion, rediscover their common Gospel roots and together grasp the beauty of their own identity in the variety of charisms with greater clarity. They should compete in mutual esteem (cf. *Rom* 12:10), striving for the greater gift, charity (cf. *1 Cor* 12:31).

Meeting and solidarity among institutes are thus encouraged, aware that "communion is closely linked to the Christian community's ability to make room for all the gifts of the Spirit. The unity of the Church is not uniformity, but an organic blending of legitimate diversities. It is the reality of many members joined in a single body, the one Body of Christ (cf. *1 Cor* 12:12)".[95]

It can be the beginning of a joint search for common ways of serving the Church. External factors, such as having to comply with the new demands of States and internal Institute factors such as the decrease in the number of members, have already led to the coordination of efforts in the fields of formation, the management of goods, education and evangelisation. Even in these situations we can find the Spirit's invitation to a more intense communion. The Conferences of Major Superiors and Conferences of Secular Institutes are to be supported at all levels in this task.

The future can no longer be faced in isolation. There is a need to be Church, to together live the adventure of the Spirit and of the following of Christ, communicating the experience of the Gospel, learning to love the other's community and religious family as one's own. The joys and sorrows, the concerns and successes belong to everyone and can be shared.

Dialogue and communion are also sought from new forms of evangelical life. These new associations of evangelical life, *Vita Consecrata* reminds us, "*are not alternatives* to already existing Institutions, which continue to hold the pre-eminent place

---

[95] *Novo Millennio Ineunte*, 46.

assigned to them by tradition... The older institutes, many of which have been tested by the severest of hardships, which they have accepted courageously down the centuries, can be enriched through dialogue and an exchange of gifts with the Foundations appearing in our own day".[96]

Finally, a new richness can spring from an encounter and communion with the charisms of ecclesial movements. Movements can often offer the example of evangelical and charismatic freshness such as the generous, creative initiatives in evangelisation. On the other hand, movements as well as new forms of evangelical life can learn a great deal from the faithful, joyful and charismatic witness of consecrated life which bears a very rich spiritual patrimony, the many treasures of experience and wisdom and a great variety of apostolates and missionary commitments.

Our Dicastery has already offered criteria and directives for the insertion of Religious men and women into ecclesial movements which are still valid.[97] What we would rather stress here is the relationship of knowledge and collaboration, of esteem and sharing which could be inserted not only among individuals but also among Institutes, ecclesial movements, and new forms of consecrated life in view of a growth in life in the Spirit and of the carrying out of the Church's one mission. It is a question of recognising which came about through the promptings of the same Spirit to bring about the fullness of evangelical life in the world, coming together to realise God's one plan for the salvation of all. The spirituality of communion is realised precisely in this vast dialogue of evangelical fraternity among all segments of the people of God.[98]

In Communion with the Laity

31. The experience of communion among consecrated persons results in an even greater openness to all other members of the Church. The command to love one another experienced in the internal life of the community must be transferred from the

---

[96] *Vita Consecrata*, 62.
[97] Cf. *Fraternal Life in Community*, 62; cf. *Vita Consecrata*, 56.
[98] Cf. *Novo Millennio Ineunte*, 45.

personal level to that of the different ecclesial realities. Only in an integrated ecclesiology, wherein the various vocations are gathered together as the one people of God, can the vocation to consecrated life once again find its specific identity as sign and witness. The fact that the charisms of founders and foundresses, having been born of the Spirit for the good of all, must once again be placed at the centre of the Church, open to communion and participation by all the People of God, is being increasingly discovered.

In this line we can see that a new type of communion and collaboration within the various vocations and states of life especially among consecrated persons and laity is beginning.[99] Monastic and contemplative Institutes can offer the laity a relationship that is primarily spiritual and the necessary spaces for silence and prayer. Institutes committed to the apostolate can involve them in forms of pastoral collaboration. Members of Secular Institutes, lay or clerical, relate to other members of the faithful at the level of everyday life.[100]

The new phenomenon being experienced in these days is that some members of the laity are asking to participate in the charismatic ideals of Institutes. This has given rise to interesting initiatives and new institutional forms of association. We are experiencing an authentic re-flourishing of ancient institutions, such as the secular orders or third orders, and the birth of new lay associations and movements linked to religious Families and Secular Institutes. Whereas at times in the recent past, collaboration came about as a means of supplementing the decline of consecrated persons necessary to carry out activities, now it is growing out of the need to share responsibility not only in the carrying out of the Institute's works but especially in the hope of sharing specific aspects and moments of the spirituality and mission of the Institute. This calls for an adequate formation of both consecrated persons and laity to ensure a collaboration which is mutually enriching.

Whereas in times past it was especially the task of religious men and women to create, spiritually nourish and direct aggregate forms

---

[99] Cf. *Fraternal Life in Community*, 70.
[100] Cf. *Vita Consecrata*, 54.

of laity, today, thanks to an every increasing formation of the laity, there can be a mutual assistance which fosters an understanding of the specificity and beauty of each state of life. Communion and mutuality in the Church are never one way streets. In this new climate of ecclesial communion, priests, religious and laity, far from ignoring each other or coming together only for a common activity, can once again find the just relationships of communion and a renewed experience of evangelical communion and mutual charismatic esteem resulting in a complimentarity which respects the differences.

This ecclesial dynamic will be helpful to the renewal and identity of consecrated life. As the understanding of the charism deepens, ever new ways of carrying it out will be discovered.

In Communion with Bishops

32. A unique aspect in this relationship of ecclesial communion with all the vocations and states of life is that of unity with Bishops. The hope of cultivating a spirituality of communion without an effective and affective relationship with the Bishops, primarily with the Pope, the center of unity of the Church and with his Magisterium, would be in vain.

It is the concrete application of *feeling with the church* proper to all the faithful[101] which especially shines in the founders and foundresses of consecrated life and which becomes the charismatic task of all Institutes. It is impossible to contemplate the face of God without seeing it shine in that of the Church. To love Christ is to love the Church in her persons and institutions.

Today, more than ever, in the face of the recurring centrifugal forces which place fundamental principles of the Catholic faith and morals in doubt, consecrated persons and their institutions are called to give proof of unity without disagreement with the Magisterium of the Church, becoming convinced and joyful spokespersons before all.

It is fitting to stress what the Pope has already affirmed in *Vita Consecrata*: "A distinctive aspect of ecclesial communion is

---

[101] Cf. *Lumen Gentium*, 12; *Vita Consecrata*, 46.

allegiance of mind and heart to the Magisterium (of the Pope and) of the Bishops, an allegiance which must be lived honestly and clearly witnessed to before the People of God by all consecrated persons, especially those involved in theological research, teaching, publishing, catechesis and the use of the means of social communications".[102] At the same time it is recognised that many theologians are Religious and many centres of research are directed by Institutes of Consecrated Life. They praiseworthily carry out this responsibility in the cultural world. The Church guards with *confident attention* their intellectual commitment in the face of the delicate front line issues which the Magisterium must face.[103]

The Church documents of the past ten years have constantly taken up the conciliar style which invites the Bishops to evaluate the specific charisms in the overall pastoral picture. At the same time they encourage consecrated persons to clearly and confidently make known and to offer their own proposals for presence and work in conformity with their specific vocation.

This also holds true, in some ways, in relationships with the Diocesan clergy. The majority of religious daily collaborate with priests in pastoral ministry. It is therefore essential to make use of all initiatives which foster greater mutual knowledge and esteem.

Only in harmony with the spirituality of communion and with the teaching outlined in *Novo Millennio Ineunte* can the Holy Spirit's gifts to the Church through the charisms of consecrated life be recognised. The coexistence in the life of the Church between the charismatic elements and the hierarchical elements which John Paul II has often mentioned when referring to new ecclesial movements[104] also holds true, in a special way, for consecrated life. Love and service in the Church must always be lived in a reciprocity of mutual charity.

---

[102] *Vita Consecrata*, 46.
[103] Cf. *Vita Consecrata*, 98.
[104] John Paul II, in *Movements in the Church*, Acts of the II International Colloquium, Milan 1987, pp.24-25; *Movements in the Church*, Vatican City 1999, p.18.

PART FOUR
WITNESSES TO LOVE

Knowing and Serving Christ

33. A life transformed by the evangelical counsels becomes a prophetic and silent witness and at the same time an eloquent protest against an inhuman world. It calls for the promotion of the individual and for a new *creativity of charity*. We have seen it in the holy founders. It is manifested not only in the effectiveness of their service but especially in their ability to identify with those who suffer in such a way that the helping hand is experienced as heartfelt sharing. This kind of evangelisation, realised through works characterised by love and dedication, ensures an unmistakable efficacy to the charity of words.[105]

In its own right, the life of communion is the first message of consecrated life, since it is an efficacious *sign* and persuasive *force* which leads to belief in Christ. Thus, communion itself is mission, indeed *"communion begets communion and is essentially a missionary communion"*.[106] Communities once again find themselves wanting to follow Christ on the paths of human history,[107] with an apostolic fervour and a witness of life which conforms to their individual charism.[108] "Those who have come into genuine contact with Christ cannot keep him for themselves, they must proclaim him. A new apostolic outreach, which will be lived *as the everyday commitment of Christian communities and groups* is needed".[109]

34. When one starts afresh from Christ the spirituality of communion becomes a strong and solid spirituality of disciples and apostles of his Kingdom. For consecrated persons this means committing themselves in service to their brothers and sisters in whom they recognise the face of Christ. In the exercise of this

---

[105] Cf. *Novo Millennio Ineunte*, 50.
[106] *Christifideles Laici*, 31-32.
[107] Cf. *Vita Consecrata*, 46.
[108] Cf. John Paul II, Apostolic Exhortation *Church in Africa*, Yaoundé, 14 September 1995, 94.
[109] *Novo Millennio Ineunte*, 40.

apostolic mission *being* and *doing* are inseparable because the mystery of Christ constitutes the absolute base for all pastoral action.[110] "The contribution of consecrated persons, both men and women, to evangelisation is, first of all, the witness of a life given totally to God and to their brothers and sisters, imitating the Saviour who, out of love for humanity, made himself a servant".[111] Consecrated persons do not limit themselves to giving only part of their time but rather give their whole life to participating in the mission of the Church.

In *Novo Millennio Ineunte*, it seems that the Pope wants to make even greater strides in concrete love for the poor. "The century and the new millennium now beginning will need to see, and hopefully with still greater clarity, to what length of dedication the Christian community can go in charity towards the poorest. If we have truly started out anew from the contemplation of Christ, we must learn to see him especially in the faces of those with whom he himself wished to be identified: 'I was hungry and you gave me food, I was thirsty and you gave me drink, I was a stranger and you welcomed me, I was naked and you clothed me, I was sick and you visited me, I was in prison and you came to me' (*Mt* 25:35-36). This Gospel text is not a simple invitation to charity, it is a page of Christology which sheds a ray of light on the mystery of Christ. By these words, no less than by the orthodoxy of her doctrine, the Church measures her fidelity as the Bride of Christ".[112] The Pope also offers a concrete direction of spirituality with the invitation to recognise in the person of the poor a *special presence* of Christ *which imposes upon the Church a preferential option for them*. It is through such an option that consecrated persons also[113] must witness to "the nature of God's love, to his providence and mercy".[114]

35. The field in which John Paul invites us to work encompasses the whole world. Facing this scenario, consecrated persons "must make their act of faith in Christ by discerning his voice in the cry

---

[110] Cf. *Novo Millennio Ineunte*, 15.
[111] *Vita Consecrata*, 76.
[112] *Novo Millennio Ineunte*, 49.
[113] Cf. *Vita Consecrata*, 82.
[114] *Novo Millennio Ineunte*, 49.

for help that rises from this world of poverty".[115] Finding the proper balance between the universal breath of a missionary vocation and its insertion into the context of a local church will be the primary challenge for all apostolic activity.

Despair at the lack of meaning in life, drug addiction, fear of abandonment in old age or sickness, marginalisation or social discrimination are new forms of poverty which have been added to its traditional forms.[116] Mission, in its traditional and new forms, is first of all a service to the dignity of the person in a dehumanised society because the greatest and most serious poverty of our time is the callous treading upon the rights of the human person. With the dynamism of charity, of forgiveness and of reconciliation, consecrated persons strive in justice to build a world which offers new and better possibilities for the life and development of the individual. Having the spirit of one who is poor, cleansed of self-interest, ready to exercise a service of peace and non-violence in a spirit of solidarity and full of compassion for the suffering of others is essential for this intervention to be effective. The way of proclaiming God's word and carrying out God's deeds, begun by Jesus (cf. *Lk* 4:15-21) and lived by the primitive Church cannot be forgotten at the end of the Jubilee or the passing of a millennium, but presses to be realised with greater urgency in charity towards a different future. One must be ready to pay the price of persecution because in our day the most frequent cause of martyrdom is the struggle for justice in faithfulness to the Gospel. John Paul affirms this witness: "even recently this has led to the martyrdom of some of your brothers and sisters in various parts of the world".[117]

In the Creativity of Charity

36. Throughout the centuries, works of charity have always provided the ambient for the concrete living out of the Gospel. In the practice of charity, consecrated persons have emphasised the prophetic nature of their charism and the richness of their

---

[115] *Novo Millennio Ineunte*, 50.
[116] Cf. *Novo Millennio Ineunte*, 50.
[117] John Paul II, *Homily* (2 February 2001): *L'Osservatore Romano*, 4 February 2001.

spirituality in the Church and in the world.[118] They recognised that they were called to be the "manifestation of God's love in the world".[119] This dynamism must continue to be exercised with creative fidelity because it constitutes an irreplaceable resource in the Church's pastoral work. At a time when a *creativity in charity* and an authentic proof and confirmation of the charity of word and action are called for,[120] consecrated life admirably safeguards the apostolic creativity which has given rise to thousands of faces of charity and holiness in specific forms; therefore, it cannot help but feel the urgency to continue, with the Spirit's creativity, to surprise the world with new forms of effective evangelical love which respond to the needs of our time.

Consecrated life has manifested the desire to reflect upon its specific charisms and its own traditions in order to place them at the service of the new boundaries of evangelisation. This means becoming one with the poor, the aged, the addicted, those suffering with AIDS, and exiled people who undergo any form of suffering because of the particular reality in which they find themselves. Attentive to the change in models, since mere assistance is no longer seen as sufficient, they seek to eradicate the causes of the needs. Poverty is caused by the ambition and indifference of many and by sinful structures which must be eliminated through a serious commitment to the field of education.

Many traditional and new foundations bring consecrated men and women to places where others usually cannot go. In recent years consecrated persons were able to leave the security of the known to thrust themselves into unknown places and works. Thanks to their total consecration they are in fact free to step in wherever there are critical needs. This has been witnessed in the recent foundations in new countries which present unique challenges, involving many provinces at the same time and creating international communities. With discerning eyes and generous hearts[121] they have responded to the call of many who suffer in a concrete service of charity. Wherever they are, they have

---

[118] Cf. *Vita Consecrata*, 84.
[119] Cf. *Vita Consecrata*, Title of Chapter III.
[120] Cf. *Novo Millennio Ineunte*, 50.
[121] Cf. *Novo Millennio Ineunte*, 58.

constituted a link between the Church and marginal groups and those not reached by ordinary pastoral ministry.

Even some charisms which seemed to have responded to times which have since passed have taken on a renewed vigour in this world which is experiencing trafficking of women and children into slavery; at the same time children, often the victims of abuse, run the risk of abandonment or conscription into armies.

Today there is a greater freedom in the exercise of the apostolates, a flourishing with greater awareness, a solidarity expressed through knowing how to stand with the people, assuming their problems, in order to respond to them, paying close attention to the signs of the times and to their needs. This multiplication of initiatives has demonstrated the importance of planning in mission if one desires to act in an ordered and efficient manner rather than haphazardly.

Announcing the Gospel

37. The first task which must be once again assumed with enthusiasm is *the proclamation of Christ to all*. This task falls especially to consecrated men and women who bring the message to the growing number of those who ignore it. This mission is still in its beginning stages and we must commit ourselves with all our resources to bring it about.[122] The confident and mutually dependent action of missionaries must always seek better ways of responding to the demands of inculturation in such a way that the specific values of each people are not rejected but purified and brought to their fullness.[123] While remaining totally faithful to the proclamation of the Gospel, Christianity of the third millennium will also be characterised by the face of the many cultures and peoples where it is taken up and rooted.[124]

---

[122] Cf. John Paul II, Encyclical *Redemptoris Missio*, Rome, 7 December 1990, 1.
[123] Cf. John Paul II, Apostolic Post-Synodal Exhortation *The Church in Asia*, New Delhi, 6 November 1999, 22.
[124] Cf. *Novo Millennio Ineunte*, 40.

Serving Life

38. Following a glorious tradition, a great number of consecrated persons, especially women, exercise their apostolate in health care ministries continuing Christ's mission of mercy. In the footsteps of the Divine Samaritan, they draw close to those who suffer, seeking to ease their pain. Their professional competence, attentively seeking to make the practice of medicine more human, gives space to the Gospel which enlightens even the most difficult experiences of human life and death with goodness and confidence. For this reason the poorest and most abandoned patients will be those who are the preferred recipients of their care.[125]

For Christian witness to be effective, it is important, especially in delicate and controversial matters, to know how to explain the reasons for the Church's position, stressing that it is not a case of imposing on non-believers a vision based on faith, but rather of interpreting and defending the values rooted in the very nature of the human person.[126] Charity, then, especially for religious who work in this ministry, is at the service of intelligence, to ensure that the fundamental principles, upon which a civilisation worthy of the human person is built, are everywhere respected.

Spreading the Truth

39. The world of education also calls for the qualified presence of consecrated men and women. The mystery of the Incarnation provides the basis for an anthropology which is capable of going beyond its own limitations and contradictions to Jesus, "the new man" (*Eph* 4:24; cf. *Col* 3:10). Because the Son of God truly became man, men and women, in and through him, can truly become children of God.[127]

Consecrated persons are able to develop a particularly incisive ministry in this field, thanks to their experience of the particular gifts of the Spirit, their careful listening to to the Word, their

---

[125] Cf. *Vita Consecrata*, 83.
[126] Cf. *Novo Millennio Ineunte*, 51.
[127] Cf. *Novo Millennio Ineunte*, 23.

constant practice of discernment and their rich heritage of pedagogical traditions amassed since the establishment of their Institutes. Equipped with this charism, consecrated persons give life to educational undertakings permeated by the Gospel spirit of freedom, justice and charity in which young people are helped to mature humanly under the action of the Spirit, while at the same time proposing sanctity as the goal of education for teachers and students alike.[128]

A *renewed cultural commitment* which seeks to raise the level of personal preparation and prepares for a dialogue between faith and the contemporary mentality, which fosters, an intense evangelisation of culture, as service to the truth, in the academic institutions themselves,[129] must be promoted in consecrated life. A presence in social communication is also needed more than ever.[130] Every effort in this new and strategic apostolic field is encouraged so that initiatives in various sectors may be better coordinated and reach higher levels of quality and effectiveness.

Openness to the Great Dialogues

40. Starting afresh from Christ means, ultimately, following him where he has made himself present in the work of salvation and living within the vast horizons opened by him. Consecrated life cannot be content living only in and for the Church. It reaches out with Christ to other Christian Churches, to other religions and to every man and woman who do not profess any religious conviction.

Consecrated life is thus called to make its specific contribution in all of the great dialogues opened to the Church by the Second Vatican Council. "Engaged in dialogue with everyone" is the significant title of the last chapter of *Vita Consecrata*, the logical conclusion to the entire Apostolic Exhortation.

41. The document recalls, above all, how the Synod on Consecrated life highlighted the close connection between consecrated life and ecumenism. "Since the soul of Ecumenism is prayer and conversion,

---

[128] Cf. *Vita Consecrata*, 96.
[129] Cf. *Vita Consecrata*, 98.
[130] Cf. *Vita Consecrata*, 99.

Institutes of Consecrated Life and Societies of Apostolic Life certainly have a special duty to foster this commitment".[131] There is an urgent need for consecrated persons to give more space in their lives to ecumenical prayer and genuine evangelical witness so that by the power of the Holy Spirit the walls of division and prejudice can be broken down. No Institute of Consecrated Life should feel itself dispensed from working for this cause.

Speaking of various forms of ecumenical dialogue, *Vita Consecrata* points out that the sharing of *lectio divina* and taking part in common prayers in which the Lord guarantees his presence (cf. *Mt* 18:20) are ways which are particularly suitable for members of religious communities. Friendship, charity and collaboration on common initiatives of service and witness will give life to the experience of how pleasant it is where brothers and sisters dwell as one (cf. *Ps* 133 [132]). Of equal importance is the knowledge of the history, doctrine, liturgy, and charitable and apostolic works of other Christians.[132]

42. *Vita Consecrata* poses two fundamental requirements for interreligious dialogue: Gospel witness and freedom of spirit. It also suggests some particular aids such as mutual knowledge, respect for one another, cordial friendship and reciprocal sincerity with monastic communities of other religions.[133]

Common concern for human life ranging from compassion for those who suffer physically and spiritually to commitment to work for peace, justice and the integrity of creation provides another area for cooperation.[134] John Paul reminds us that a particular field for successful common action with people of other religious traditions is that of the search for and promotion of the dignity of women which consecrated women are called to contribute to in a special way.[135]

43. Finally, the dialogue with those who do not profess any religious belief is brought to mind. Consecrated persons, by the very nature of their choice, become privileged partners in the

---

[131] *Vita Consecrata*, 100.
[132] Cf. *Vita Consecrata*, 101.
[133] Cf. *Ecclesia in Asia*, 31, 34.
[134] Cf. *The Church in Asia*, 44.
[135] Cf. *Vita Consecrata*, 102.

search for God which has always stirred the human heart and has led to the different forms of asceticism and spirituality. Their sensitivity to values (cf. *Phil* 4:8) and their willingness to meet give witness to the characteristics of an authentic search for God. "For this reason", the document concludes, "consecrated persons are in duty bound to offer a generous welcome and spiritual support to all those who, moved by a thirst for God and a desire to live the demands of faith, turn to them".[136]

44. This dialogue necessarily opens up to the proclamation of Christ. In communion there is a mutual gifting. An authentic listening to the other provides the proper occasion to share one's own spiritual experiences and their evangelical content which nourish consecrated life. Thus we give witness to the hope that is within us (cf. *1 Peter* 3:15). We should not fear that speaking of our own faith might be seen as an offense to someone who professes a different belief. It is rather an occasion for the joyful proclamation of the gift which is for all and is offered to all with the greatest respect for each person's freedom, the gift of revelation of the God of Love who "so loved the world to give his only Son" (*Jn* 3:16).

The missionary obligation, on the other hand, does not stop us from entering into dialogue with others fully open to receive, since from among the resources and limits of every culture consecrated persons can gather the *seeds of the Word* in which they encounter precious values for their life and mission. "The Spirit of God who 'blows where he wills' (*Jn* 3:8) not infrequently reveals signs of his presence which help Christ's followers to understand more deeply the message which they bear".[137]

The Daily Challenges

45. It is not possible to remain indifferent to the prospect of an ecological crisis which is making vast areas of our planet uninhabitable and hostile to humanity. The rich countries are consuming resources at a rate which cannot sustain the equilibrium of the system, thus causing

---

[136] Cf. *Vita Consecrata*, 103.
[137] *Novo Millennio Ineunte*, 56.

poor countries to become even poorer. Nor can one forget the problems of peace so often threatened by the spectre of catastrophic wars.[138]

Greed, the craving of pleasure, the idolatry of power, the triple concupiscence which marks history and is also at the root of present evils can only be overcome if the Gospel values of poverty, chastity and service are rediscovered.[139] Consecrated persons must know how to proclaim, with their lives and with their words, the beauty of poverty of spirit and of chastity of heart which free one for service to brothers and sisters and of obedience which gives longevity to the fruits of charity.

How can we remain passive in the face of contempt for fundamental human rights?[140] A special commitment must be made to certain radical aspects of the Gospel which are often less understood but which cannot, because of this, be given less importance in the Church's agenda of charity. First among these is the respect for every human life from the moment of conception to natural death.

In this openness to the world which must be ordered to Christ in such a way that all realities find their true meaning in him, consecrated lay men and women who are members of Secular Institutes hold a privileged position. Sharing the common conditions of life, they effectively work for the Kingdom of God by participating in the political and social reality bringing to them a new value, in view of their following of Christ. Precisely through their consecration lived without external signs, as lay people among lay people, they can be *salt and light* even in those situations in which a visible sign of consecration would be rejected or serve as an impediment.

Looking Forward and Beyond

46. "Sentinels of the Dawn": young men and women are also found among consecrated persons.[141] We truly need courageous young people who, allowing themselves to be configured by the Father with the work of the Spirit and becoming "persons conformed to

---

[138] Cf. *Novo Millennio Ineunte*, 51.
[139] Cf. *Vita Consecrata*, 88-91.
[140] Cf. *Novo Millennio Ineunte*, 51.
[141] Cf. *Novo Millennio Ineunte*, 9.

Christ",[142] offer to all a joyful and transparent witness of their "specific acceptance of the mystery of Christ"[143] and of the particular spirituality of their own Institute.[144]

May they therefore be seen more decisively as protagonists of their own formation.[145] Since, for generational motives, they will have to carry on the renewal of their own institutes, it is fitting that-following an adequate preparation-they gradually assume guiding and governing tasks. Strengthened by their spark of idealism they become true witnesses to the striving for holiness, to the *high standard* of Christian living.[146] The future of consecrated life and its mission rests in a large part on the strength of their faith, on the attitudes which they have joyfully manifested and on what the Spirit wishes to tell them.

Let us look upon Mary, Mother and Teacher of all. She, the first consecrated person, lived the fullness of charity. Fervent in the Spirit, she served the Lord, joyful in hope, strong in trial, persevering in prayer; she intercedes for us (cf. *Rom* 12:11-13). She reflects all the aspects of the Gospel; all the charisms of consecrated life are mirrored and renewed in her. She supports us in our daily commitments, making them a splendid witness of love in accord with the invitation of St Paul: "Live a life worthy of the calling you have received!" (*Eph* 4:1).

We once again turn to the words of John Paul II to confirm these orientations, because in them we find the encouragement and confidence which we all need to face the task which seems beyond our strength: "A new century, a new millennium are opening in the light of Christ. But not everyone can see this light. Ours is the wonderful and demanding task of becoming its *'reflection'*... This is a daunting task if we consider our human weakness, which so often renders us opaque and full of shadows. But it is a task which we can accomplish if we turn to the light of

---

[142] *Vita Consecrata*, 19.
[143] *Vita Consecrata*, 16.
[144] Cf. *Vita Consecrata*, 93.
[145] Cf. Congregation for Institutes of Consecrated Life and Societies of Apostolic Life, *Potissimum Institutioni*, Rome, 2 February 1990, 29.
[146] Cf. *Novo Millennio Ineunte*, 31.

Christ and open ourselves to the grace which makes us a new creation".[147] This is the hope proclaimed in the Church by consecrated men and women as through the centuries, with their brothers and sisters, they encounter the Risen Christ.

On May 16, 2002 the Holy Father approved this Document of the Congregation for Institutes of Consecrated Life and Societies of Apostolic Life.

Rome, 19 May 2002, The Solemnity of Pentecost.

Eduardo Card. Martínez Somalo
Prefect

Piergiorgio Silvano Nesti, CP
Secretary

---

[147] Cf. *Novo Millennio Ineunte*, 54.